SOFT CURRENCY ECONOMICS II

WHAT EVERYONE THINKS THEY KNOW ABOUT MONETARY POLICY IS WRONG

By Warren Mosler

All Rights Reserved. No part of this publication may be reproduced in any form or by any means, including scanning, photocopying, or otherwise without prior written permission of the copyright holder.

Copyright © 1996 & 2012 Valance Company, Inc.

Valance Economics

Valance Company, Inc.
5013 Chandlers Wharf, Suite 2
Christiansted, USVI 00820
Office phone: (340) 692-7710 (fax 7715)

For More Information visit

www.softcurrencyeconomics.com

The Next Book in the Series

Warren Mosler; The 7 Deadly Innocent Frauds of Economic Policy

TABLE OF CONTENTS

PREFACE 1
TWENTY YEARS AGO - AN ITALIAN EPIPHANY 4
SOFT CURRENCY ECONOMICS 11
    Statement of Purpose 13
    Fiat Money 16
    The Myth of the Money Multiplier 23
    The Myth of Debt Monetization 26
    How Fed Funds Targeting fits into Overall Monetary
    Policy 27
    Mechanics of Federal Spending 29
    Federal Government Spending, Borrowing and Debt 33
    Interest Rate Maintenance Account (IRMA) 34
    Fiscal Policy Options 34
    The Gold System as a Basis for Reserves 36
    Reserve Requirements, History, Rationale & Current
    Practice 40
    The Discount: History & Operation 43
    Failure to Meet Reserve Requirements 47
    The Fed Funds Market 47
    The Repurchase Agreements Market (Repos) 49
    Matched Sales Purchases 50
    The Fed in the Repo Market 51
    Controlling the Fed Funds Rate 54
    Further Discussion of Inelasticity 57
    Lead Accounting 59
    More on Why Lead Accounting is Unworkable – Inelasticity
    for Loan Demand 60

What if No One Buys the Debt 62
How the Government Spends and Borrows as Much
as it Does Without Causing Hyperinflation 63
Full Employment and Price Stability...66
Taxation...68
Foreign Trade 69
Inflation vs. Price Increase..70
Conclusion...72

MOSLER SPEECH - ROME DEBT MANAGEMENT CONFERENCE OCTOBER 26, 2012 74
OTHER RECOMMENDED BOOKS.............................81
APPENDIX FOR SOFT CURRENCY ECONOMICS..........82
BIBLIOGRAPHY FOR SOFT CURRENCY ECONOMICS 83
ABOUT THE AUTHOR 85

Preface

Soft Currency Economics was first published after the author, Warren Mosler, founder of Illinois Income Investors (which later became the top ranking III investment companies), triggered an Italian Epiphany in Rome in 1992. He met with the Professor Luigi Spaventa, a senior official of the Italian Government's Treasury Department, to discuss why Italian government bonds were trading at a steep discount to Italian corporate bonds. At the time, the discount existed because the perception was that Italy, not the large Italian corporations, was more likely to default on its debt. This was contrary to Mosler's understanding of fiat currencies. He was convinced that a sovereign with its own free trading currency could never default on its debt unless the government decided to default.

Mosler had Spaventa validate and confirm his thinking that the market had the pricing all wrong. This lead to very successful trades for Mosler, what he referred to a "free 2%" return, and at the same time educated Spaventa that Italy (this was prior to the Euro) could not go bankrupt unless it wanted to, and thus Italy did not have to succumb to the pressure from the IMF to implement austerity programs.

The Italian Epiphany subsequently led to the publication of Soft Currency Economics in 1996. This book became the cornerstone for a heterodox economic theory that is today known as Modern Monetary Theory or MMT. The book explains how the monetary system and banks operate in contrast to what is taught in most of today's college textbooks.

It is often said that history repeats itself. Twenty years after the Italian Epiphany, Italy is once again experiencing financial difficulties and there is once again a discussion of the potential for default. One major difference exists today compared to the early 1990s and that is the monetary system that existed in the 1990s no longer applies. Today, Italy no longer has its own free trading fiat currency that it can issue to pay government expenditures. Instead, Italy now has to borrow Euros to fund expenditures and it is the European Central Bank (ECB), not the Italian Central Bank, which can provide the economic remedy.

At the Debt Public Management conference in Rome on October 26, 2012 which included Mario Draghi (head of the ECB), Mosler proposed the following three strategies to address the problems in many the European economies:

1. A tax credit bond, which is a bond that in the case of nonpayment can be used directly for the payment of taxes;

2. An ECB guarantee of national government debt and an expansion of Maastricht limits to perhaps 7% of GDP to trigger an immediate surge of sales; and/or

3. For the ECB to make 'cash' distributions to the member nations on a per capita basis of perhaps 10% of euro zone GDP annually.

Subsequent to this conference, and with a growing understanding by the Italian population that Italy can have better control of its economy with its own currency, currency determination versus austerity became an issue in the February 2013 election, which saw outsider Beppe Grillo and his Five Star Movement, a brand new political party, received 8.7 million votes and have the potential to control a coalition government.

This re-publication of Soft Currency Economics has two new additions. It includes Mosler's personal recollection of his Italian Epiphany as well as the speech he presented at the Debt Public Management conference.

Russell Huntley, Editor

Twenty Years Ago - An Italian Epiphany

Circumstances in the early 1990's led me to an understanding of the actual functioning of a currency. Back then, it was the government of Italy, rather than the United States, which was in crisis. Professor Rudi Dornbusch, an influential academic economist at MIT, insisted that Italy was on the verge of default because their debt-to-GDP ratio exceeded 110% and the lira interest rate was higher than the Italian growth rate.

Things were so bad that Italian Government Securities denominated in lira yielded about 2% more than the cost of borrowing the lira from the banks. The perceived risk of owning Italian government bonds was so high that you could buy Italian government securities at about 14%, and borrow the lira to pay for them from the banks at only about 12% for the full term of the securities. This was a free lunch of 2%, raw meat for any bond desk like mine, apart from just one thing; the perceived risk of default by the Italian government. There was easy money to be made, but only if you knew for sure that the Italian government wouldn't default.

The "Free Lunch" possibility totally preoccupied me. The reward for turning this into a risk free spread was immense. So I started brainstorming the issue with my partners. We knew no nation had ever defaulted on its own currency when it was not legally convertible into gold or anything else. There was a time when nations issued securities that were convertible into gold. That era, however, ended for good in 1971 when President Nixon took us off the gold standard internationally (the same year I got my BA from U-Conn) and we entered the era of floating exchange rates and non-convertible currencies.

While some people still think that the America dollar is backed by the gold in Fort Knox, which is not the case. If you take a $10 bill to the Treasury Department and demand gold for it, they won't give it to you because they simply are not legally allowed to do so, even if they wanted to. They will give you two $5 bills or ten $1 bills, but forget about getting any gold.

Historically, government defaults came only with the likes of gold standards, fixed exchange rates, external currency debt, and indexed domestic debt. But why was that? The answer generally given was "because they can always print the money." Fair enough, but there were no defaults (lots of inflation but no defaults) and no one ever did "print the money," so I needed a better reason before committing millions of our investors funds.

A few days later when talking to our research analyst, Tom Shulke, it came to me. I said, "Tom, if we buy securities from the Fed or Treasury, functionally there is no difference. We send the funds to the same place (the Federal Reserve) and we own the same thing, a Treasury security, which is nothing more than account at the Fed that pays interest."

So functionally it has to all be the same. Yet presumably the Treasury sells securities to fund expenditures, while when the Fed sells securities, it's a "reserve drain" to "offset operating factors" and manage the fed funds rate. Yet they have to be functionally the same - it's all just a glorified reserve drain! Many of my colleagues in the world of hedge fund management were intrigued by the profit potential that might exist in the 2% free lunch that the Government of Italy was offering us. Maurice Samuels, then a portfolio manager at Harvard Management, immediately got on board, and set up meetings for us in Rome with officials of the Italian government to discuss these issues.

Maurice and I were soon on a plane to Rome. Shortly after landing, we were meeting with Professor Luigi Spaventa, a senior official of the Italian Government's Treasury Department. (I recall telling Maurice to duck as we entered the room. He looked up and started to laugh. The opening was maybe twenty feet high. "That's so you could enter this room in Roman times carrying a spear," he replied.) Professor Spaventa was sitting behind an elegant desk. He was wearing a three-piece suit, and smoking one of those curled pipes. The image of the great English economist John Maynard Keynes, whose work was at the center of much economic policy discussion for so many years, came to mind. Professor Spaventa was Italian, but he spoke English with a British accent, furthering the Keynesian imagery.

After we exchanged greetings, I opened with a question that got right to the core of the reason for our trip. "Professor Spaventa, this is a rhetorical question, but why is Italy issuing Treasury securities? Is it to get lira to spend, or is it to prevent the lira interbank rate falling to zero from your target rate of 12%?" I could tell that Professor Spaventa was at first puzzled by the questions. He was probably expecting us to question when we would get our withholding tax back. The Italian Treasury Department was way behind on making their payments. They had only two people assigned to the task of remitting the withheld funds to foreign holders of Italian bonds, and one of these two was a woman on maternity leave.

Professor Spaventa took a minute to collect his thoughts. When he answered my question, he revealed an understanding of monetary operations we had rarely seen from Treasury officials in any country. "No," he replied. "The interbank rate would only fall to 1/2%, NOT 0%, as we pay 1/2% interest on reserves." His insightful response was everything we had hoped for. Here was a Finance Minister who actually understood monetary operations and reserve accounting! (Note also that only recently has the U.S. Fed been allowed to pay interest on reserves as a tool for hitting their interest rate target).

I said nothing, giving him more time to consider the question. A few seconds later he jumped up out of his seat proclaiming "Yes! And the International Monetary Fund is making us act pro cyclical!" My question had led to the realization that the IMF was making the Italian Government tighten policy due to a default risk that did not exist.

Our meeting, originally planned to last for only twenty minutes, went on for two hours. The good Professor began inviting his associates in nearby offices to join us to hear the good news, and instantly the cappuccino was flowing like water. The dark cloud of default had been lifted. This was time for celebration!

A week later, an announcement came out of the Italian Ministry of Finance regarding all Italian government bonds - "No extraordinary measures will be taken. All payments will be made on time." We and our clients were later told we were the largest holders of Italian lira denominated bonds outside of Italy, and managed a pretty good few years with that position.

Italy did not default, nor was there ever any solvency risk. Insolvency is never an issue with non-convertible currency and floating exchange rates. We knew that, and now the Italian Government also understood this and was unlikely to "do something stupid," such as proclaiming a default when there was no actual financial reason to do so. Over the next few years, our funds and happy clients made well over $100 million in profits on these transactions, and we may have saved the Italian Government as well. The awareness of how currencies function operationally inspired this book and hopefully will soon save the world from itself.

As I continued to consider the ramifications of government solvency not being an issue, the ongoing debate over the U.S. budget deficit was raging. It was the early 1990's, and the recession had driven the deficit up to 5% of GDP (deficits are traditionally thought of as a percent of GDP when comparing one nation with another, and one year to another, to adjust for the different sized economies).

Gloom and doom were everywhere. News anchor David Brinkley suggested that the nation needed to declare bankruptcy and get it over with. Ross Perot's popularity was on the rise with his fiscal responsibility theme. Perot actually became one of the most successful 3rd party candidates in history by promising to balance the budget. (His rising popularity was cut short only when he claimed the Viet Cong were stalking his daughter's wedding in Texas.)

With my new understanding, I was keenly aware of the risks to the welfare of our nation. I knew that the larger federal deficits was what was fixing the broken economy, but I watched helplessly as our mainstream leaders and the entire media clamored for fiscal responsibility (lower deficits) and were prolonging the agony.

It was then that I began conceiving the academic paper that would become Soft Currency Economics. I discussed it with my previous boss, Ned Janotta, at William Blair.

He suggested I talk to Donald Rumsfeld (his college roommate, close friend and business associate), who personally knew many of the country's leading economists, about getting it published. Shortly after, I got together with "Rummy" for an hour during his only opening that week. We met in the steam room of the Chicago Racquet Club and discussed fiscal and monetary policy. He sent me to Art Laffer who took on the project in 1994 and assigned Mark McNary to co-author, research and edit. Soft Currency Economics, which follows was published in 1996.

Soft Currency Economics

In the midst of great abundance our leaders promote privation. We are told that national health care is unaffordable, while hospital beds are empty. We are told that we cannot afford to hire more teachers, while many teachers are unemployed. And we are told that we cannot afford to give away school lunches, while surplus food goes to waste.

When people and physical capital are employed productively, government spending that shifts those resources to alternative use forces a trade-off. For example, if thousands of young men and women were conscripted into the armed forces the country would receive the benefit of a stronger military force. However, if the new soldiers had been home builders, the nation may suffer a shortage of new homes. This trade-off may reduce the general welfare of the nation if Americans place a greater value on new homes than additional military protection. If, however, the new military manpower comes not from home builders but from individuals who were unemployed, there is no trade-off. The real cost of conscripting home builders for military service is high; the real cost of employing the unemployed is negligible.

The essence of the political process is coming to terms with the inherent trade-offs we face in a world of limited resources and unlimited wants. The idea that people can improve their lives by depriving themselves of surplus goods and services contradicts both common sense and any respectable economic theory. When there are widespread unemployed resources as there are today in the United States, the trade-off costs are often minimal, yet mistakenly deemed unaffordable.

When a member of Congress reviews a list of legislative proposals, he currently determines affordability based on how much revenue the federal government wishes to raise, either through taxes or spending cuts. Money is considered an economic resource. Budget deficits and the federal debt have been the focal point of fiscal policy, not real economic costs and benefits. The prevailing view of federal spending as reckless, disastrous and irresponsible, simply because it increases the deficit, prevails.

Interest groups from both ends of the political spectrum have rallied around various plans designed to reduce the deficit. Popular opinion takes for granted that a balanced budget yields net economic benefits only to be exceeded by paying off the debt. The Clinton administration claims a lower 1994 deficit as one of its highest achievements. All new programs must be paid for with either tax revenue or spending cuts. Revenue neutral has become synonymous with fiscal responsibility.

The deficit doves and deficit hawks who debate the consequences of fiscal policy both accept traditional perceptions of federal borrowing. Both sides of the argument accept the premise that the federal government borrows money to fund expenditures. They differ only in their analysis of the deficit's effects. For example, doves may argue that since the budget does not discern between capital investment and consumption expenditures, the deficit is overstated. Or, that since we are primarily borrowing from ourselves, the burden is overstated. But even if policy makers are convinced that the current deficit is a relatively minor problem, the possibility that a certain fiscal policy initiative might inadvertently result in a high deficit, or that we may owe the money to foreigners, imposes a high risk. It is believed that federal deficits undermine the financial integrity of the nation.

Policy makers have been grossly misled by an obsolete and non-applicable fiscal and monetary understanding. Consequently, we face continued economic under-performance.

Statement of Purpose

The purpose of this work is to clearly demonstrate, through pure force of logic, that much of the public debate on many of today's economic issues is invalid, often going so far as to confuse costs with benefits. This is not an effort to change the financial system. It is an effort to provide insight into the fiat monetary system, a very effective system that is currently in place.

The validity of the current thinking about the federal budget deficit and the federal debt will be challenged in a way that supersedes both the hawks and the doves. Once we realize that the deficit can present no financial risk, it will be evident that spending programs should be evaluated on their real economic benefits, and weighed against their real economic costs. Similarly, a meaningful analysis of tax changes evaluates their impact on the economy, not the impact on the deficit. It will also be shown that taxed advantaged savings incentives are creating a need for deficit spending.

The discussion will begin with an explanation of fiat money, and outline key elements of the operation of the banking system. The following points will be brought into focus:

> ***Monetary Policy Sets the Price of Money***, which only indirectly determines the quantity. It will be shown that the overnight interest rate is the primary tool of monetary policy. The Federal Reserve sets the overnight interest rate, the price of money, by adding and draining reserves. Government spending, taxation, and borrowing can also add and drain reserves from the banking system and, therefore, are part of that process.
>
> ***The Money Multiplier Concept Is Backwards***. Changes in the money supply cause changes in bank reserves and the monetary base, not vice versa.
>
> ***Debt Monetization Cannot and Does Not Take Place***.
>
> ***The Imperative behind Federal Borrowing Is to Drain Excess Reserves*** *from the banking*

system, to support the overnight interest rate. It is not to fund untaxed spending. Untaxed government spending (deficit spending), as a matter of course, creates an equal amount of excess reserves in the banking system. Government borrowing is a reserve drain, which functions to support the fed funds rate mandated by the Federal Reserve Board of Governors.

The Federal Debt Is Actually An Interest Rate Maintenance Account (IRMA).

Fiscal Policy Determines the Amount of New Money directly created by the federal government. Briefly, deficit spending is the direct creation of new money. When the federal government spends and then borrows, a deposit in the form of a treasury security is created. The national debt is essentially equal to all of the new money directly created by fiscal policy.

Options Over Spending, Taxation, And Borrowing, However, Are Not Limited by the process itself but by the desirability of the economic outcomes. The amount and nature of federal spending as well as the structure of the tax code and interest rate maintenance (borrowing) have major economic ramifications. The decision of how much money to borrow and how much to tax can be based on the economic effect of varying the mix, and need not focus solely on the mix itself (such as balancing the budget).

Finally, the conclusion will incorporate five additional discussions.

What If No One Buys The Debt?

- How the government manages to spend as much as it does and not cause hyper-inflation.
- Full employment AND price stability.
- Taxation and a discussion of foreign trade.

Fiat Money

Historically, there have been three categories of money: commodity, credit, and fiat. Commodity money consists of some durable material of intrinsic value, typically gold or silver coin, which has some value other than as a medium of exchange. Gold and silver have industrial uses as well as an esthetic value as jewelry. Credit money refers to the liability of some individual or firm, usually a checkable bank deposit.

FIAT MONEY IS A TAX CREDIT NOT BACKED BY ANY TANGIBLE ASSET.

In 1971 the Nixon administration abandoned the gold standard and adopted a fiat monetary system, substantially altering what looked like the same currency. Under a fiat monetary system, money is an accepted medium of exchange only because the government requires it for tax payments.

Government fiat money necessarily means that federal spending need not be based on revenue. The federal government has no more money at its disposal when the federal budget is in surplus, than when the budget is in deficit. Total federal expense is whatever the federal government chooses it to be. There is no inherent financial limit. The amount of federal spending, taxing and borrowing influence inflation, interest rates, capital formation, and other real economic phenomena, but the amount of money available to the federal government is independent of tax revenues and independent of federal debt. Consequently, the concept of a federal trust fund under a fiat monetary system is an anachronism. The government is no more able to spend money when there is a trust fund than when no such fund exists. The only financial constraints, under a fiat monetary system, are self-imposed.

The concept of fiat money can be illuminated by a simple model: Assume a world of a parent and several children. One day the parent announces that the children may earn business cards by completing various household chores. At this point the children won't care a bit about accumulating their parent's business cards because the cards are virtually worthless. But when the parent also announces that any child who wants to eat and live in the house must pay the parent, say, 200 business cards each month, the cards are instantly given value and chores begin to get done. Value has been given to the business cards by requiring them to be used to fulfill a tax obligation. Taxes function to create the demand for federal expenditures of fiat money, not to raise revenue per se. In fact, a tax will create a demand for at LEAST that amount of federal spending. A balanced budget is, from inception, the MINIMUM that can be spent, without a continuous deflation. The children will likely desire to earn a few more cards than they need for the immediate tax bill, so the parent can expect to run a deficit as a matter of course.

To illustrate the nature of federal debt under a fiat monetary system, the model of family currency can be taken a step further. Suppose the parent offers to pay overnight interest on the outstanding business cards (payable in more business cards). The children might want to hold on to some cards to use among themselves for convenience. Extra cards not needed overnight for inter-sibling transactions would probably be deposited with the parent. That is, the parent would have borrowed back some of the business cards from the children. The business card deposits are the national debt that the parent owes.

The reason for the borrowing is to support a minimum overnight lending rate by giving the holders of the business cards a place to earn interest. The parent might decide to pay (support) a high rate of interest to encourage saving. Conversely, a low rate may discourage saving. In any case, the amount of cards lent to the parent each night will generally equal the number of cards the parent has spent, but not taxed - the parent's deficit. Notice that the parent is not borrowing to fund expenditures, and that offering to pay interest (funding the deficit) does not reduce the wealth (measured by the number of cards) of each child.

In the U. S., the 12 members of the Federal Open Market Committee decide on the overnight interest rate. That, along with what Congress decides to spend, tax, and borrow (that is, pay interest on the untaxed spending), determines the value of the money and, in general, regulates the economy.

Federal borrowing and taxation were once part of the process of managing the Treasury's gold reserves. Unfortunately, discussions about monetary economics and the U. S. banking system still rely on many of the relationships observed and understood during the time when the U. S. monetary regime operated under a gold standard, a system in which arguably the government was required to tax or borrow sufficient revenue to fund government spending. Some of the old models are still useful in accurately explaining the mechanics of the banking system. Others have outlived their usefulness and have led to misleading constructs. Two such vestiges of the gold standard are the role of bank reserves (including the money multiplier) and the concept of monetization. An examination of the workings of the market for bank reserves reveals the essential concepts. (Additional monetary history and a more detailed explanation are provided in the appendix).

The Fed defines the method that banks are required to use in computing deposits and reserve requirements. The period which a depository institution's average daily reserves must meet or exceed its specified required reserves is called the reserve maintenance period. The period in which the deposits on which reserves are based are measured is the reserve computation period. The reserve accounting method was amended in 1968 and again in 1984 but neither change altered the Fed's role in the market for reserves.

Before 1968 banks were required to meet reserve requirements contemporaneously: reserves for a week had to equal the required percentage for that week. Banks estimated what their average deposits would be for the week and applied the appropriate required reserve ratio to determine their reserve requirement. The reserve requirement was an obligation each bank was legally required to meet. Bank reserves and deposits, of course, continually change as funds are deposited and withdrawn which confounded the bank manager's task of managing reserve balances. Because neither the average deposits for a week nor the average amount of required reserves could be known with any degree of certainty until after the close of the last day it was "like trying to hit a moving target with a shaky rifle." Therefore, in September 1968, lagged reserve accounting (LRA) replaced contemporaneous reserve accounting (CRA). Under LRA the reserve maintenance period was seven days ending each Wednesday (see Figure 1). Required reserves for a maintenance period were based on the average daily reservable deposits in the reserve computation period ending on a Wednesday two weeks earlier. The total amount of required reserves for each bank and for the banking system as a whole was known in advance. Actual reserves could vary, but at least the target was stable.

Figure 1 - The Lagged Reserve Accounting System, 1968-1984

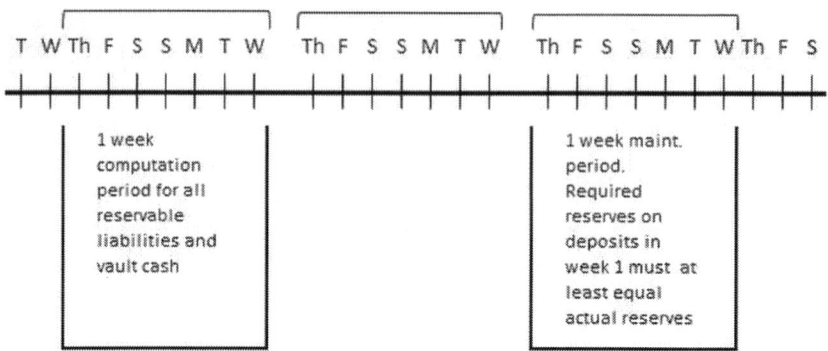

In 1984 the Board of Governors of the Federal Reserve System reinstated CRA. The reserve accounting period is now two weeks (see Figure 2). Reserves on the last day of the accounting period are one-fourteenth of the total to be averaged. For example, if a bank borrowed $7 billion for one day it would currently add 1/14 of $7 billion, or $500 million, to the average level of reserves for the maintenance period. Although this system is called contemporaneous it is, in practice, a lagged system because there is still a two-day lag: reserve periods end on Wednesday but deposit periods end on the preceding Monday. Thus even under CRA the banking system is faced with a fixed reserve requirement as it nears the end of each accounting period.

The 1984 adoption of CRA occurred as federal officials, economists, and bankers debated whether shortening the reserve accounting lag could give the Fed control of reserve balances. The change was consciously designed to give the Fed direct control over reserves and changes in deposits. Federal Reserve Chairman Volcker favored the change to CRA in the mistaken belief that a shorter lag in reserve accounting would give the Fed greater control over reserves and hence the money supply. Chairman Volcker was mistaken. The shorter accounting lag did not (and could not) increase the Fed's control over the money supply because depository institutions reserve requirements are based on total deposits from the previous accounting period. Banks for all practical purposes cannot change their current reserve requirements.

Figure 2 - The lagged Reserve Accounting System, 1984 to present

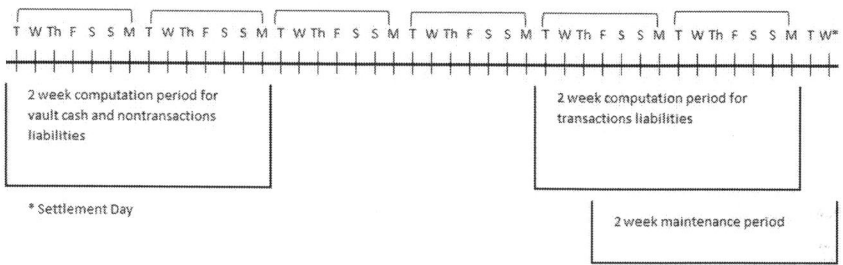

Under both CRA and LRA the Fed must provide enough reserves to meet the known requirements, either through open market operations or through the discount window. If banks were left on their own to obtain more reserves no amount of interbank lending would be able to create the necessary reserves. Interbank lending changes the location of the reserves but the amount of reserves in the entire banking system remains the same. For example, suppose the total reserve requirement for the banking system was $60 billion at the close of business today but only $55 billion of reserves were held by the entire banking system. Unless the Fed provides the additional $5 billion in reserves, at least one bank will fail to meet its reserve requirement. The Federal Reserve is, and can only be, the follower, not the leader when it adjusts reserve balances in the banking system.

The role of reserves may be widely misunderstood because it is confused with the role of capital requirements. Capital requirements set standards for the quality and quantity of assets which banks hold on the quality of its loans. Capital requirements are designed to insure a minimum level of financial integrity. Reserve requirements, on the other hand, are a means by which the Federal Reserve controls the price of funds which banks lend. The Fed addresses the quantity and risk of loans through capital requirements; it addresses the overnight interest rate by setting the price of reserves.

The Myth of the Money Multiplier

Everyone who has studied money and banking has been introduced to the concept of the money multiplier. The multiplier is a factor which links a change in the monetary base (reserves + currency) to a change in the money supply. The multiplier tells us what multiple of the monetary base is transformed into the money supply (M = m x MB). Since George Washington's portrait first graced the one dollar bill students have listened to the same explanation of the process. No matter what the legally required reserve ratio was, the standard example always assumed 10 percent so that the math was simple enough for college professors. What joy must have spread through the entire financial community when, on April 12, 1992, the Fed, for the first time, set the required reserve ratio at the magical 10 percent. Given the simplicity and widespread understanding of the money multiplier it is a shame that the myth must be laid to rest. The truth is the opposite of the textbook model.

> **IN THE REAL WORLD, BANKS MAKE LOANS INDEPENDENT OF RESERVE POSITIONS, AND THEN DURING THE NEXT ACCOUNTING PERIOD, THEY BORROW ANY NEEDED RESERVES. THE IMPERATIVES OF THE ACCOUNTING SYSTEM, AS PREVIOUSLY DISCUSSED, REQUIRE THE FED TO LEND TO THE BANKS WHATEVER THEY NEED.**

Bank managers generally neither know nor care about the aggregate level of reserves in the banking system. Bank lending decisions are affected by the price of reserves, not by reserve positions. If the spread between the rate of return on an asset and the fed funds rate is wide enough, even a bank deficient in reserves will purchase the asset and cover the cash needed by purchasing (borrowing) money in the funds market. This fact is clearly demonstrated by many large banks when they consistently purchase more money in the fed funds market than their entire level of required reserves. These banks would actually have negative reserve levels if not for fed funds purchases i.e. borrowing money to be held as reserves.

If the Fed should want to increase the money supply, devotees of the money multiplier model (including numerous Nobel Prize winners) would have the Fed purchase securities. When the Fed buys securities reserves are added to the system. However, the money multiplier model fails to recognize that the added reserves in excess of required reserves drive the funds rate to zero, since reserve requirements do not change until the following accounting period. That forces the Fed to sell securities, i.e., drain the excess reserves just added, to maintain the funds rate above zero.

If, on the other hand, the Fed wants to decrease money supply, taking reserves out of the system when there are no excess reserves places some banks at risk of not meeting their reserve requirements. The Fed has no choice but to add reserves back into the banking system, to keep the funds rate from going, theoretically, to infinity.

In either case, the money supply remains unchanged by the Fed's action. The multiplier is properly thought of as simply the ratio of the money supply to the monetary base ($m = M/MB$). Changes in the money supply cause changes in the monetary base, not vice versa. The money multiplier is more accurately thought of as a divisor ($MB = M/m$).

Failure to recognize the fallacy of the money-multiplier model has led even some of the most well-respected experts astray. The following points should be obvious, but are rarely understood:

> 1. THE INELASTIC NATURE OF THE DEMAND FOR BANK RESERVES LEAVES THE FED NO CONTROL OVER THE QUANTITY OF MONEY. THE FED CONTROLS ONLY THE PRICE.
>
> 2. THE MARKET PARTICIPANTS WHO HAVE DIRECT AND IMMEDIATE EFFECT ON THE MONEY SUPPLY INCLUDE EVERYONE EXCEPT THE FED.

The Myth of Debt Monetization

The subject of debt monetization frequently enters discussions of monetary policy. Debt monetization is usually referred to as a process whereby the Fed buys government bonds directly from the Treasury. In other words, the federal government borrows money from the Central Bank rather than the public. Debt monetization is the process usually implied when a government is said to be printing money. Debt monetization, all else equal, is said to increase the money supply and can lead to severe inflation. However, fear of debt monetization is unfounded, since the Federal Reserve does not even have the option to monetize any of the outstanding federal debt or newly issued federal debt.

> AS LONG AS THE FED HAS A MANDATE TO MAINTAIN A TARGET FED FUNDS RATE, THE SIZE OF ITS PURCHASES AND SALES OF GOVERNMENT DEBT ARE NOT DISCRETIONARY.

Once the Federal Reserve Board of Governors sets a fed funds rate, the Fed's portfolio of government securities changes only because of the transactions that are required to support the funds rate. The Fed's lack of control over the quantity of reserves underscores the impossibility of debt monetization. The Fed is unable to monetize the federal debt by purchasing government securities at will because to do so would cause the funds rate to fall to zero. If the Fed purchased securities directly from the Treasury and the Treasury then spent the money, its expenditures would be excess reserves in the banking system. The Fed would be forced to sell an equal amount of securities to support the fed funds target rate. The Fed would act only as an intermediary. The Fed would be buying securities from the Treasury and selling them to the public. No monetization would occur.

To monetize means to convert to money. Gold used to be monetized when the government issued new gold certificates to purchase gold. In a broad sense, federal debt is money, and deficit spending is the process of monetizing whatever the government purchases. Monetizing does occur when the Fed buys foreign currency. Purchasing foreign currency converts, or monetizes, that currency to dollars. The Fed then offers U.S. Government securities for sale to offer the new dollars just added to the banking system a place to earn interest. This often misunderstood process is referred to as sterilization.

How Fed Funds Targeting fits into Overall Monetary Policy

The Federal Reserve is presumed to conduct monetary policy with the ultimate goal of a low inflation and a monetary and financial environment conducive to real economic growth. The Fed attempts to manage money and interest rates to achieve its goals. It selects one or more intermediate targets, because it believes they have significant effects on the money supply and the price level.

Whatever the intermediate targets of monetary policy may be, the Fed's primary instrument for implementing policy is the federal funds rate. The fed funds rate is influenced by open market operations. It is maintained or adjusted in order to guide the intermediate target variable. If the Fed is using a quantity rule (i.e., trying to determine the quantity of money), the intermediate target is a monetary aggregate such as M1 or M2. For instance, if M2 grows faster than its target rate the Fed may raise the fed funds rate in an effort to slow the growth rate of M2. If M2 grows too slowly the Fed may lower the fed funds rate. If the Fed chooses to use the value of money as its intermediate target then the fed funds target will be set based on a price level indicator such as the price of gold or the Spot Commodities Index. Under a price rule the price of gold, for example, is targeted within a narrow band. The Fed raises the fed funds rate when the price exceeds its upper limit and lowers the rate when the price falls below its lower limit in hopes that a change in the fed funds rate returns the price of gold into the target range.

Open market operations offset changes in reserves caused by the various factors which affect the monetary base, such as changes in Treasury deposits with the Fed, float, changes in currency holdings, or changes in private borrowing. Open market operations act as buffers around the target fed funds rate. The target fed funds rate may go unchanged for months. In 1993, the target rate was held at 3 percent without a single change. In other years the rate was changed several times.

Mechanics of Federal Spending

The federal government maintains a cash operating balance for the same reason individuals and businesses do; current receipts seldom match disbursements in timing and amount. The U. S. Treasury holds its working balances in the 12 Federal Reserve Banks and pays for goods and services by drawing down these accounts. Deposits are also held in thousands of commercial banks and savings institutions across the country. Government accounts at commercial banks are called Tax and Loan accounts because funds flow into them from individual and business tax payments and proceeds from the sale of government bonds. Banks often pay for their purchases of U. S. Treasury securities or purchases on behalf of their customers by crediting their Tax and Loan accounts.

The Treasury draws all of its checks from accounts at the Fed. The funds are transferred from the Tax and Loan accounts to the Fed then drawn from the Fed account to purchase goods and services or make transfer payments. Suppose the Treasury intends to pay $500 million for a B-2 stealth bomber. The Treasury transfers $500 million from its Tax and Loan accounts to its account at the Fed. The commercial banks now have $500 million less in deposits and hence $500 million less reserves. At the Fed, reserves decrease by $500 million while Treasury deposits have increased by $500 million. At this instant the increase in U. S. Treasury deposits reduces reserves and the monetary base but when the Treasury pays for the bomber the preceding process is reversed. U. S. Treasury deposits at the Fed fall by $500 million and the defense contractor deposits the check received from the Treasury in its bank, whose reserves rise by $500 million. Government spending does not change the monetary base when reserves move simultaneously in equal amounts and opposite directions.

Figures 3 and 4 compare the T-accounts of the banking system, the Treasury and the Federal Reserve for a $500 million expenditure. Figure 3 shows the net change for an expenditure offset by tax receipts. Figure 4 shows the net change when the expenditure is offset by borrowing. In either case reserve balances are left unchanged. There is no net change in the banking system when the bomber is paid for with tax receipts. When the Treasury issues securities to pay for the bomber, deposits in the banking system increase by $500 million. The Federal Reserve's use of offsetting open market operations to keep the funds rate within its prescribed range is primarily applied to changes in government deposit balances.

Figure 3 - The Government Spends $500 million and Taxes $500 million

SPEND

Banking System

Assets		Liabilities	
Reserves	+500	Deposits	+500

U.S. Treasury

Assets		Liabilities	
Deposits at Fed	-500		
Taxes Due	+500		

Federal Reserve

Assets		Liabilities	
		Reserves	+500
		Treas Deposits.	-500

TAX

Banking System

Assets		Liabilities	
Reserves	-500	Deposits	-500

U.S. Treasury

Assets		Liabilities	
Deposits at Fed	+500		
Item Purchased	-500		

Federal Reserve

Assets		Liabilities	
		Reserves	-500
		Treas Deposits.	+500

NET CHANGE

Banking System

Assets		Liabilities	
Reserves	0	Deposits	0

U.S. Treasury

Assets		Liabilities	
Deposits at Fed	0	Deposits	+500
Taxes Due	-500		
Bomber	+500		

Federal Reserve

Assets		Liabilities	
		Reserves	0
		Treas Deposits.	0

Figure 4 - The Government Spends $500 million and borrows $500

SPEND

Banking System
Assets		Liabilities	
Reserves	+ 500	Deposits	+ 500

U.S. Treasury
Assets		Liabilities	
Deposits at Fed	- 500		
Item Purchased	+500		

Federal Reserve
Assets		Liabilities	
		Reserves	+ 500
		Treas Deposits.	- 500

BORROW

Banking System
Assets		Liabilities	
Reserves	- 500		

U.S. Treasury
Assets		Liabilities	
Deposits at Fed	+ 500	Securities	+ 500

Federal Reserve
Assets		Liabilities	
		Reserves	- 500
		Treas Deposits.	+ 500

NET CHANGE

Banking System
Assets		Liabilities	
Reserves	0		
Securities	+ 500		

U.S. Treasury
Assets		Liabilities	
Bomber	+ 500	Securites	+ 500

Federal Reserve
Assets		Liabilities	
		Reserves	0
		Treas Deposits.	0

Federal Government Spending, Borrowing and Debt

The Fed's desire to maintain the target fed funds rate links government spending, which adds reserves to the banking system, and government taxation and borrowing, which drain reserves from the banking system.

> **UNDER A FIAT MONETARY SYSTEM, THE GOVERNMENT SPENDS MONEY AND THEN BORROWS WHAT IT DOES NOT TAX, BECAUSE DEFICIT SPENDING, IF NOT OFFSET BY BORROWING, WOULD CAUSE THE FED FUNDS RATE TO FALL.**

The Federal Reserve does not have exclusive control of reserve balances. Reserve balances can be affected by the Treasury itself. For example, if the Treasury sells $100 of securities, thereby increasing the balance of its checking account at the Fed by $100, reserves decline just as if the Fed had sold the securities. When either government entity sells government securities reserve balances decline. When either buys government securities (in this case the Treasury would be retiring debt) reserves in the banking system increase. The monetary constraints of a fed funds target dictate that the government cannot spend money without borrowing (or taxing), nor can the government borrow (or tax) without spending. The financial imperative is to keep the reserve market in balance, not to acquire money to spend.

Interest Rate Maintenance Account (IRMA)

Over the course of time the total number of dollars that have been drained from the banking system to maintain the fed funds rate is called the federal debt. A more appropriate name would be the Interest Rate Maintenance Account (IRMA). The IRMA is simply an accounting of the total amount of securities issued to pay interest on untaxed money spent by the government.

Consider the rationale behind adjusting the maturities of government securities. Since the purpose of government securities is to drain reserves from the banking system and support an interest rate, the length, or maturity, of the securities is irrelevant for credit and rollover purposes. In fact, the IRMA could consist entirely of overnight deposits by member banks of the Fed, and the Fed could support the fed funds rate by paying interest on all excess reserves. One reason for selling long-term securities might be to support long-term interest rates.

Fiscal Policy Options

The act of government spending and concurrent taxation gives the illusion that the two are inextricably linked. The illusion is strengthened by the analogy of government as a business or government as a household. Businesses and households in the private sector are limited in how much they may borrow by the market's willingness to extend credit. They must borrow to fund expenditures.

> THE FEDERAL GOVERNMENT, ON THE OTHER HAND, IS ABLE TO SPEND A VIRTUALLY UNLIMITED AMOUNT FIRST, ADDING RESERVES TO THE BANKING SYSTEM, AND THEN BORROW, IF IT WISHES TO CONDUCT A RESERVE DRAIN.

Each year Congress approves a budget outlining federal expenditures. Congress also decides how to finance those expenditures; in fiscal 1993 for example, government expenditures were $1.5 trillion. The financing was made up of $1.3 trillion in tax receipts and $0.2 trillion in borrowing. The total revenue must equal total expenditures to maintain control of the fed funds rate. The composition of the total revenue between taxes and borrowing is at the discretion of Congress. The economic impact of varying the composition of government financing between taxes and borrowing is worthy of much research, discussion and debate. Unfortunately, sober discussion of the deficit's economic implications has been dominated by apocalyptic sermons on the evils of deficit spending *per se*.

Since the federal budget deficit became an issue in the early eighties the warnings abound over the severe consequences of partaking in the supposedly sinister practice of borrowing money from the private sector. Enough warnings about the federal deficit have been made by Democrats, Republicans and other patriotic Americans to fill a new wing in the Smithsonian. The following is but a small sample:

> *"The national deficit is like cancer. The sooner we act to restrict it the healthier our*

-35-

fiscal body will be and the more promising our future." **Senator Paul Simon** *(D-IL).*

"...because of the manner in which our debt has been financed, we are at great risk if interest rates rise dramatically, or even moderately. The reason is that over 70 percent of the publicly- held debt is financed for less than five years. That's suicide in business, that's suicide in your personal life, and that's suicide in your government." **Ross Perot***.*

"Our nation's wealth is being drained drop by drop, because our government continues to mount record deficits...The security of our country depends on the fiscal integrity of our government, and we're throwing it away." **Senator Warren Rudman***.*

"...a blow to our children's living standards." **The New York Times***.*

"...this great nation can no longer tolerate running runaway deficits and exorbitant annual interest payments..." **Senator Howell T. Heflin, (D-AL)***.*

The Gold System as a Basis for Reserves

The gold standard was established in the U. S. in 1834. Under a gold standard the price of gold is set in terms of the dollar. The dollar was defined as 23.22 fine grains of gold. With 480 grains to the fine troy ounce, this was equivalent to $20.67 per ounce. The monetary authority was then committed to keep the mint price of gold fixed by being willing to buy or sell the gold in unlimited amounts.

The gold standard was suspended from 1861 to 1879 due to the Civil War. The variant which prevailed in the U. S. from 1880 to 1914 was a fractional reserve gold coin standard. Under that standard both government issued notes and notes issued by commercial banks (also deposits) circulated alongside gold coins. These forms of currency were each convertible on demand into gold. Gold reserves were held by the issuers to maintain convertibility.

In 1934 the Gold Reserve Act devalued the dollar by increasing the monetary price of gold from $20.67 to $35.00 an ounce. The Act put the U. S. on a limited gold bullion standard under which redemption in gold was restricted to dollars held by foreign central banks and licensed private users.

As a domestic monetary standard, gold reserves regulated the domestic money supply. In a fractional reserve gold standard the money supply was determined by the monetary gold stock and the ratio of the monetary gold stock to the total money supply which consisted of gold coins, fiduciary notes and bank deposits. Money creation was determined by the amount of gold reserves. Bank deposits depended on 1) the level of gold reserves held by commercial banks and the central bank, 2) the preferences of the public for gold coins relative to other forms of money, and 3) legal gold reserve ratios.

The primary attraction of gold as a basis for a monetary system is that its supply is limited, or at least increases slowly, whereas fiat money is limited only by the judgments of presumably fallible people. While the gold standard provided a stable monetary framework during much of its reign as the prevailing world monetary standard, the gold standard itself is not immune to problems of inflation and deflation. For example, an increase in the gold supply brought about by a major gold strike could increase prices and disrupt financial markets.

Under gold standard rules and regulations, gold set the ultimate barrier to the expansion of bank reserves and the supply of Federal Reserve Notes. Gold set the upper limit to liabilities of the Federal Reserve Banks. For example, in 1963 the note and deposit liabilities of the Federal Reserve Banks could not exceed four times their holdings of gold certificates, a special form of currency backed 100 percent by gold actually held in the Treasury vaults at Fort Knox, Kentucky. If the total Federal Reserve Bank liabilities were $50 billion then a least $12.5 billion of the total would have to be in gold certificates. If the Fed were to reach the upper limit the Fed would be unable to purchase any more government securities on balance or to increase loans to member banks. This would mean that bank reserves could no longer increase and would even have to shrink if the public wished to hold more currency. In this case the upper limit in the money supply would have been reached. If a further increase in the money supply appeared desirable the Fed had two options. First, the Federal Reserve could lower the banks' requirements so that with the same volume of reserves banks could lend larger sums. Second, the Board of Governors of the Federal Reserve System could suspend the 25 percent gold certificate reserve requirement.

The actual movement of gold into and out of the Treasury was a unique process because of the status of gold as a monetary standard. A description of the process of acquiring gold explains how gold certificates found their way into Federal Reserve Banks. The term "monetize" means that the Treasury simply creates new money when they acquire gold. When the Treasury wished to purchase a gold brick from a gold mine they printed a gold certificate.

In the actual process of monetizing gold the Treasury buys it from a gold mine. The gold bars are delivered to Fort Knox. The government pays by issuing a check. The gold mine deposits the check in its commercial bank. The commercial bank, in turn sends the check to the Federal Reserve Bank for deposit to its reserve account there. The Reserve Bank then reduces the Treasury's balance by the amount of the check. The original outlay by the government has increased the gold mine's account without reducing any other private account in the commercial banking system, and, the commercial bank has gained reserves while no other bank has lost reserves. In effect, the Treasury's balance at the Federal Bank has been shifted to a commercial bank. Both the money supply and commercial bank reserves have been increased.

Note that this type of government spending which increases reserves and the money supply is unique to the purchase of gold under a gold standard. When the government buys anything other than gold they have to have, so to speak, money in the bank to pay for it. The money the government spends on missiles, cement, paper clips or the President's salary has to be raised by taxation or by borrowing. The government, like everyone else, is prohibited from simply printing money to pay for the things it buys. If the government assigned other commodities the role held by gold only then would the government acquire cement or paper clips by printing cement certificates or paper clip certificates. Everything else on which the government spends is covered by taxes or borrowing. Therefore, expenditures by the government from its account at the Fed are continuously offset by receipts of taxes or borrowed funds.

Reserve Requirements, History, Rationale & Current Practice

Laws requiring banks and other depository institutions to hold a certain fraction of their deposits in reserve, in very safe, secure, assets have been part of the U. S. banking system since 1863, well before the establishment of the Federal Reserve System in 1913. Prior to the existence of the Fed, reserve requirements were thought to help ensure the liquidity of bank notes and deposits. But as bank runs and financial panics continued periodically, it became apparent that reserve requirements did not guarantee liquidity. The notion of reserve requirements as a source of liquidity vanished completely upon creation of the Federal Reserve System as lender of last resort.

Since 1913 there have been two primary roles associated with reserve requirements: money control and a revenue source for the Treasury. The Federal Reserve has viewed reserve requirements as a mechanism to stabilize the money supply. The Fed has sought to set reserve requirements as part of the process of controlling the money supply. The Fed's objective is to control the supply of reserves. In the theory based on the gold standard an increase in the amount of reserves provided to the banking system should be associated with an increase in reservable deposits in an amount that is a multiple of the reserve increase. (Today, however, banks make loans independent of their position. This critical departure will be discussed later.)

Reserve requirements also result in an implicit tax on banks because reserves held at the Fed do not earn interest. Therefore, reserve requirements reduce the revenues of the member banks. The burden of a given level of reserve requirement depends heavily on the level of nominal interest rates: the higher the rates the greater the earnings foregone. The magnitude of the reserve tax has varied considerably over the last several years. When the nominal interest rate soared to over 10 percent in the early 1980s foregone interest reached $4 billion per year.

In the fourth quarter of 1992 the effective tax was at a rate of $700 million per year. Although the amount of the reserve tax has declined in recent years as nominal interest rates have fallen the impact of the reserve tax depends on the effective rate of taxation rather than the total amount. The higher the effective tax rate on banks the lower the net return on loans.

As implied by basic tax theory, the higher the rate of taxation on the production of any product the greater will be the price paid by the demanders of that product and the lower will be the price received by the suppliers of that product. Taxes introduce a wedge between prices paid and prices received. Borrowers pay more and banks receive less for loans. A simple way in which the Fed could eliminate the reserve tax on banks is to pay interest on the reserves. If the Fed paid a market-based rate of interest on required reserve balances, the reserve tax would essentially be eliminated as would the distortion of the tax on resource allocation. In the past, proposals to pay interest on required reserve balances have encountered resistance because they would reduce the earnings remitted by the Fed to the Treasury.

The reserve tax has always discouraged membership in the Federal Reserve System. To reduce the burden of the tax, legislation was enacted to allow banks to use vault cash to satisfy their reserve requirements. This change was phased-in beginning December 1959. At the end of 1992, 56 percent of required reserve balances were in the form of vault cash. Despite the efforts of the Federal Reserve System the membership declined steadily. In 1959 approximately 85 percent of all transaction deposits were at member banks. By 1980 the portion of transaction deposits at member banks had fallen to less than 65 percent.

In response to declining membership the Fed sought changes, other than the elimination of the reserve tax, to prevent membership attrition from further undermining the efficacy of monetary policy. In 1980 Congress adopted legislation to reform the reserve requirement rules. The Monetary Control Act of 1980 mandated universal reserve requirements to be set by the Federal Reserve for all depository institutions, regardless of their membership status. The act also simplified the reserve requirement schedule.

The Discount: History & Operation

The role of the discount window changed considerably between the founding of the Federal Reserve in 1913 and the 1930s as open market operations gradually replaced discount window borrowing as the primary source of Federal Reserve credit. Then, between 1934 and 1950 the discount window fell into disuse. Since the creation of the Fed, Regulation A has set the procedures that banks must follow to gain access to the discount window. Reserve banks may lend to depository institutions either through advances secured by U. S. government securities or by discounting paper of acceptable quality such as mortgage notes, local government securities and commercial paper. The rate on the loans from Federal Reserve banks to depository institutions is set administratively by the Fed. The Board of Governors initiates a discount rate and the 12 regional Federal Reserve Banks adopt it within a two-week period. Although we speak of the discount rate there are actually several rates depending on the collateral offered by the borrower.

Each Federal Reserve Bank's board of directors sets its discount rates subject to approval of the Board of Governors. Since the 1950s the Fed's stated policy discourages persistent reliance on borrowing. Borrowing from the discount window is supposed to represent only a modest share of total reserves. The actual amount of borrowed reserves is total reserves demanded by the banking system minus the amount of unborrowed reserves provided by the Fed through open market operations. Officially the Fed fashions the discount window as a safety valve, a temporary source of resources when they are not readily available from other sources. The discount window is simply a means of accommodating the reserve requirements of the banking system - the same reserves provided through open market operations but with a slightly different price and slightly different packaging. Both the 1980 and 1990 versions of Regulation A state as a general requirement that "Federal Reserve credit is not a substitute for capital." But all along, fed policy has determined the amount of borrowing. To the extent that immediate reserve needs are not provided through open market purchases they must be provided through the discount window. In this context the window's role is in meeting known reserve needs.

Throughout its history the Fed has used the discount window for much more than its stated purpose. To accommodate Treasury financing needs in World War I, the Reserve Banks were empowered to extend direct collateral loans to member banks. Continuous borrowing year in and year out was not uncommon in the 1920s. The availability of the discount window was expanded in 1932 by the Emergency Relief and Construction Act. The act opened the discount window to non-banks. It permitted the Reserve Banks to lend to individuals, partnerships and corporations, with no other source of funds or notes eligible for discount at member banks. The Act of June 19, 1934 authorized Reserve Banks to make advances to established commercial or industrial enterprises for the purpose of supplying working capital if the borrower was unable to attain assistance from the usual sources. It is unclear whether the Act had any impact on the net amount of lending. Essentially, Federal Reserve Banks were authorized to make loans on behalf of the taxpayers. When a Federal Reserve Bank made a direct business loan the loan created a new deposit in the banking system. The new deposit added bank reserves which could be used to purchase government bonds from the Fed. The net change to the banking system's balance sheet was an increase in deposits matched by an increase in government securities. Reserve Banks continued to make and co-finance working capital industrial loans until authorization to do so was repealed by the Small Business Investment Act of 1958.

Since the 1980s, Federal Reserve lending to institutions with a high probability of insolvency in the near term represents a major departure from its historic mandate to provide loans to illiquid, but not insolvent, banks. A study conducted at the request of the House Banking Committee collected data on all depository institutions that borrowed funds from the discount window from January 1, 1985 through May 10, 1991. Regulators grade banks on their performance according to a scale of 1 to 5. The grades are based on five measures known by the acronym CAMEL, for Capital Adequacy, Asset Quality, Management, Earnings, and Liquidity. The Federal Reserve reported that of 530 borrowers that failed within three years of the onset of their borrowings, 437 were classified as most problem-ridden with a CAMEL rating of 5, the poorest rating; 51 borrowers had the next lowest rating, CAMEL 4. At the time of failure 60 percent of the borrowers had outstanding discount window loans. These loans were granted almost daily to institutions with a high probability of insolvency.

The Fed's use of the discount window has expanded to cover a wide range of reserve needs. The frequency of borrowing from the discount window has no explicit restrictions. The banks using the discount window are not held to any financial strength standards. The de facto criterion for eligibility for discount loans is simply need. Experience has consistently shown that the Fed will not allow a bank to fail when a bank requires a loan to cover its reserve requirement. The cost of discount borrowing may vary considerably as the discount rate changes and as administrative costs and/or penalties change. Nevertheless, the discount window remains accessible to any bank's reserve needs.

The Fed's allocation of borrowed reserves as a percent of total reserves has been less than 1 percent since 1986. Since 1950 borrowed reserves have fluctuated from near zero to as high as 6-1/2 percent of total reserves. The bank failures during the mid-eighties heightened the public's awareness of discount window borrowing as a sign, accurate or not, of fiscal weakness. Banks have become more hesitant to go to the window so as to not damage their reputation.

Failure to Meet Reserve Requirements

Another form of borrowed reserves occurs when a bank has a reserve deficiency. If a bank fails to meet its reserve requirement it is subject to a reserve-deficiency charge. Reserve banks are authorized to assess charges at a rate of 2% above the discount rate. Thus, the Fed provides a third minor source of reserves for banks unable to acquire the required level of reserves from the fed funds market or the discount window.

The Fed Funds Market

The Fed funds market is a means by which banks can obtain funds from other banks or nonbank lenders such as U. S. government agencies, savings and loan associations, mutual savings banks, or an agency or branch of a foreign bank. Federal funds are unsecured bank loans. Federal funds do not belong to the federal government as the name might suggest. Fed funds are not subject to reserve requirements; they are, in effect, reserves traded among financial institutions.

Member banks have reserves in the Fed which are also known as immediately available funds since they can be transferred almost instantaneously over Fedwire. Fedwire is the Federal Reserve's system that electronically transfers funds and securities on its communications network. Money and securities are no more than accounting data. A bank can access its account at its Reserve Bank to transfer funds or securities to any other depository institution that has a Reserve Bank account. When banks borrow fed funds they are actually borrowing deposits from other banks. The transfer of fed funds increases the deposits at the borrowing bank and reduces deposits at the lending bank. Most fed funds borrowing is for one day; essentially these borrowings are one-day unsecured loans.

Banks could obtain funds by selling Treasury bills, either outright or as reverse repos, but for one day or a few days such sales are less convenient and slightly more costly than fed funds. No matter what the method of acquiring funds, bank reserves are simply transferred from one bank to another. Interbank reserve transactions change the location of reserves but do not alter the total amount of reserves held in the banking system.

Banks may obtain funds in the fed funds market to maintain their reserve requirement. They have lines of credit with each other to enact direct transfers of funds. Banks have been known to borrow fed funds continuously and in excess of their reserve requirement when it is profitable to do so. Banks may borrow beyond their reserve requirement and lend the borrowed funds at higher rates than the cost of borrowing. The difference between a bank's cost of money and the return on loans determines its willingness to lend. The cost of money defines the cost of loans, and thus the demand for loans.

The Repurchase Agreements Market (Repos)

The transfer of funds is also facilitated by the market for repurchase agreements (the repo market). Banks use repurchase agreements (RPs) to obtain short-term funds or as a means of investing funds on a very short-term basis. Banks are the temporary recipients of funds; other banks or the Fed may supply funds. RPs are quite flexible; they can be issued for one day or they may be continuing contracts. In an overnight repurchase agreement, a security, such as a U. S. Treasury bill, is purchased from a bank which agrees to repurchase the security at the same price plus interest the next day. In effect the 'buyer' is making a loan to the bank.

Repurchase agreements may also be made by corporations or individuals. For example, a large corporation such as General Motors may have some idle funds in its bank account, say, $1 million, which it would like to lend overnight. GM uses this excess $1 million to buy Treasury bills from a bank which agrees to repurchase them the next morning at a price slightly higher than GM's purchase price. The effect of this agreement is that GM makes a loan of $1 million to the bank and holds $1 million of the bank's Treasury bills until the bank repurchases the bills to pay off the loan. Commercial banks often provide corporate depositors with sweep accounts which automatically invest deposits in overnight RPs. Although the checking account does not legally pay interest, in effect the corporation is receiving interest on balances that are available for writing checks.

Since 1969 repurchase agreements have developed into an important source of funds for banks. The volume of RPs exceeds $140 billion. The interest on RPs is not determined by the interest on the Treasury bill used as collateral but rather by the interest in the market for repos which is closely associated with the fed funds rate. Since repos have collateral and federal funds do not, the repo rate is generally a little lower than the fed funds rate.

While the trading has its eye on the funds rate the actual open market transactions are made in the repo market. The Fed is thereby able to manage the fed funds rate within a reasonably narrow band.

Matched Sales Purchases

Matched-sale purchase transactions (MSPs) have been used since 1966. MSPs, also known as reverse RPs, allow the Fed to sell securities (Borrow money) with an agreement to repurchase them (pay off the loan) within a short time. The use of MSPs is preferred to direct sales followed later by purchases because of the temporary nature of the market for reserves. For example, an increase in the float that temporarily increases reserves may result when transportation facilities are halted by a snowstorm. The excess reserves may be temporarily reduced by MSPs.

The Fed in the Repo Market

Occasionally the Fed conducts open market operations by carrying out straight forward purchases or sales of securities, but these outright transactions are rare. At the New York Fed's trading desk where open market operations are executed, the desk executes outright security transactions only when it perceives a permanent change in reserve needs. In 1992 the desk entered the market to buy securities outright only six times.

Ordinarily, the New York Fed's trading desk arranges self-reversing transactions to meet temporary reserve needs. The great bulk of the purchases are done under repurchase agreements in the repo market. While most of the Fed's security sales are executed by MSPs (also known as reverse repos), with the Fed pledging to buy these securities back at a particular time. When the funds rate rises above the desired level more reserves for the banking system are needed. The Fed uses repos to buy securities, adding reserves to the system until the funds rate falls back to the desired level. When the funds rate dips below the prescribed rate the Fed sells securities with reverse repos, which drain reserves from the banking system, until the funds rate climb to the target rate. The Fed uses the repo market to manage the daily level of reserves in the banking system because open market operations are intended to affect reserves for only a very short time. Repo transactions enable the Fed to offset the many market fluctuations which change the amount of reserves. The Fed does not need to know the exact nature of a monetary disturbance, by watching the fed funds rate the Fed knows when to offset any shock in the money market with open market operations.

The desk's activity is shown graphically in Figures 5 and 6 Fed economist Joshua Feinman tracked daily transactions of the open market desk from June 1988 through December 1990.

Figure 5 - Probabilities of the Open Market Desk Daily Transactions June 1998 to December 1990

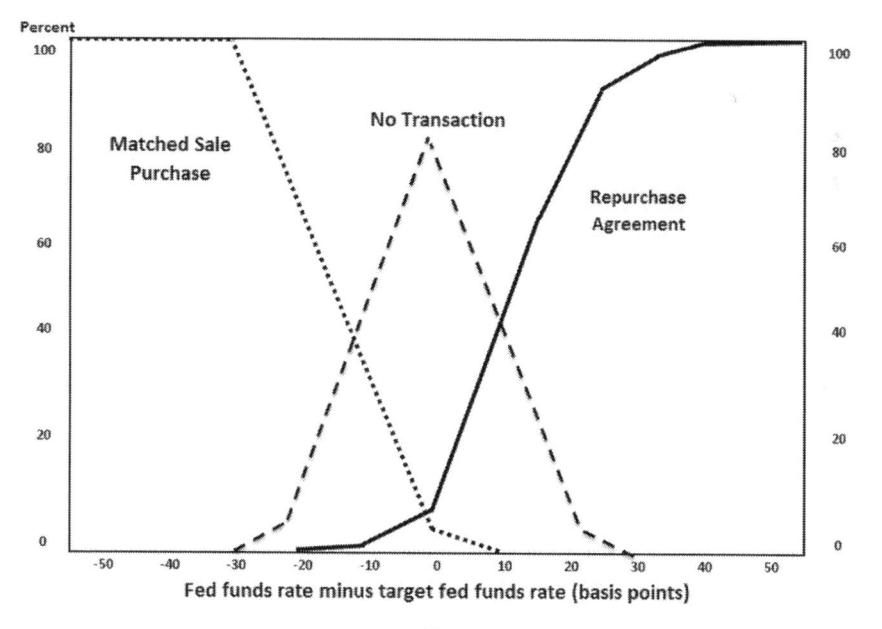

Figure 6 depicts the likelihood of the desk's use of RPs and MSPs in the repo market. The graph also plots the probability that the desk will abstain from participating in the market.

Figure 6 - Likelihood that the Fed's Desk uses Repurchase and Reverse Repos

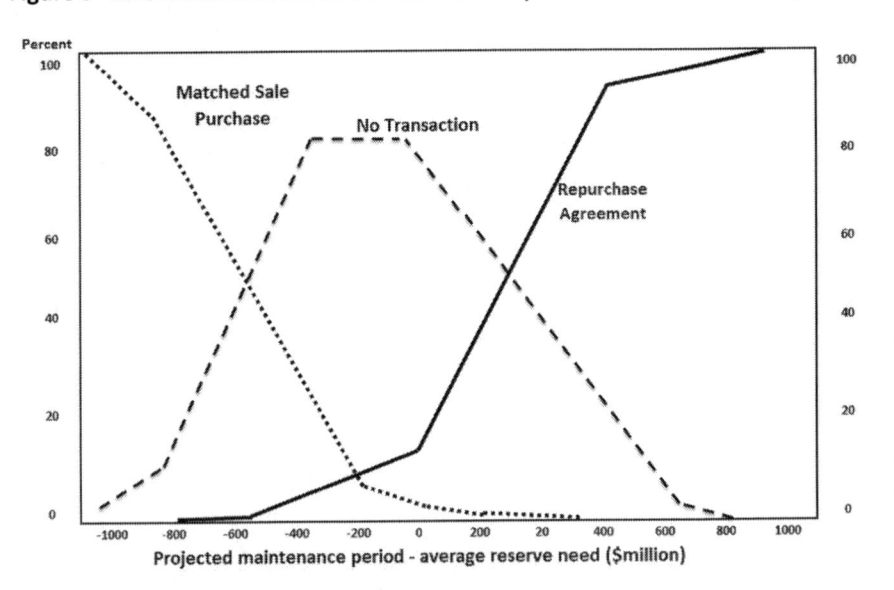

[Graph: Percent (y-axis, 0-100) vs. Projected maintenance period - average reserve need ($million) (x-axis, -1000 to 1000). Shows three curves: Matched Sale Purchase (dotted, high on left), No Transaction (dashed, peaks in middle), and Repurchase Agreement (solid, high on right).]

Figures 5 and 6 also shows the probability of the desk's use of RPs and MSPs based upon the average reserve need of the banking system. Note the slight bias of the no transaction line. The desk is somewhat more willing to allow a reserve deficiency to persist than an equal amount of reserve excess. The presence of the discount window as a source of reserves accounts for the desk's slightly smaller aversion to reserve deficiency versus reserve excess.

Using the fed funds rate as its daily guide the Fed uses open market operations continuously to stabilize the funds rate. In theory and in practice the trading desk has an easy task. Once the desired fed funds rate has been determined, conducting offsetting open market operations is as simple as driving a car within the bounds of a straight, clearly marked lane. When the vehicle starts to drift a minor adjustment is made to correct its path, if the vehicle drifts in the opposite direction the driver uses the opposite correction.

Controlling the Fed Funds Rate

The supply of reserves consists of three parts: vault currency, reserves supplied through fed open market transactions, and loans from the Fed's discount window (Figure 7).

To the extent the Fed leaves the banking system short of reserves through open market operations, banks short of reserves try to borrow from each other and bid up the fed funds rate. As the spread between the fed funds rate and the discount rate widens more banks will borrow from the discount window. Borrowing from the discount window carries some administrative costs as well as a stigma of financial weakness. Nevertheless, as the funds rate rises higher and higher above the discount rate more banks will go to the window. Banks are, after all, profit making businesses and the financial incentives to borrow from the window increase as the spread between the funds rate and the discount rate widens.

Figure 7 - Supply and demand curve for Reserves

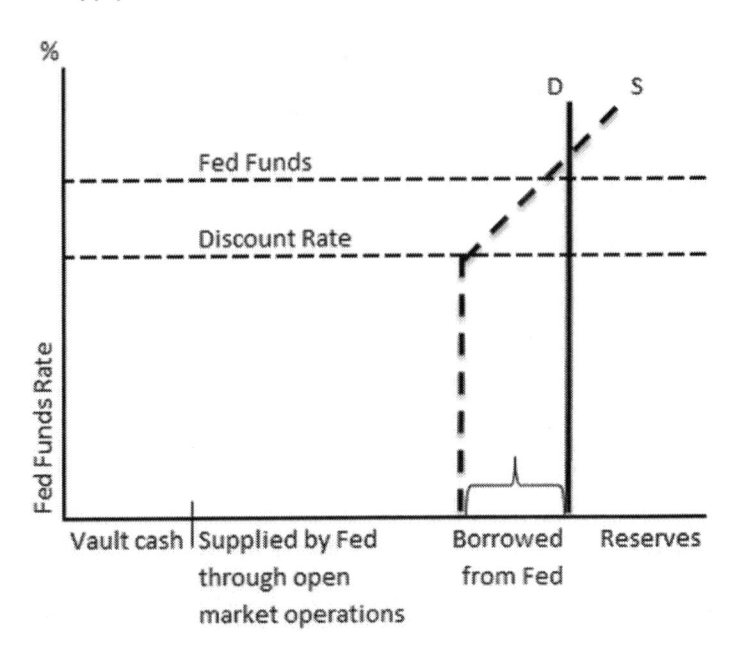

Figure 8 shows that when interest rates on fed funds rise above the discount rate, depository institutions borrow from the Fed. In other words, the Fed supplies the needed resources to the banking system by purchasing securities in the open market or lending at the discount window. By adjusting the composition of the reserves between borrowed and non-borrowed the Fed sets the spread between the fed funds and the discount rate. The Fed uses open market operations to adjust reserve balances so as to keep the banking system in a net borrowed position. To reduce the spread between the fed funds rate and the discount rate the Fed provides more unborrowed reserves through open market purchases. To increase the spread the Fed provides fewer unborrowed reserves which require banks to bid up the price of fed funds and borrow more heavily from the discount window.

Figure 8 - Supply and Demand Curves for Reserves

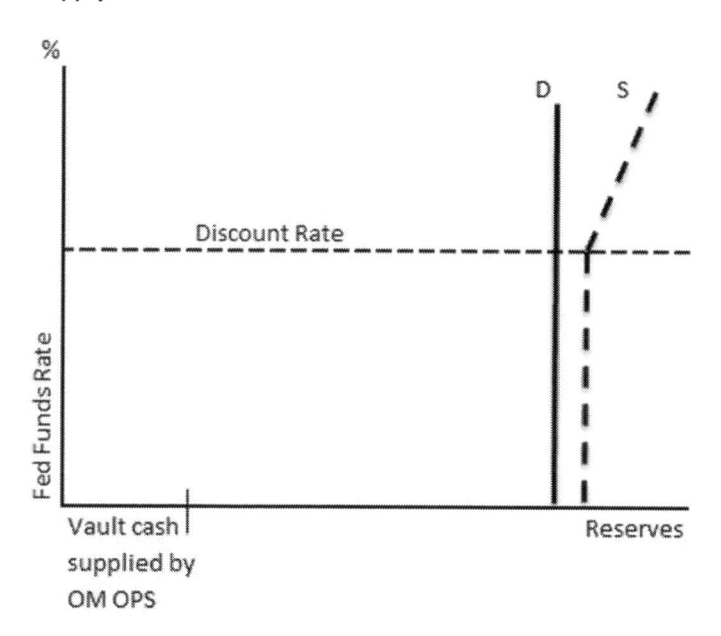

The fed funds rate is closely watched by the trading desk of the Federal Reserve Bank of New York as the indicator of the reserve position of the banking system. Every depository institution with a reserve requirement ends its reporting period and must come up with its required reserves (an average for the period) by the close of business on every other Wednesday. A perceived surplus sends the funds rate plummeting downward; an expected shortage sends the rate shooting upward. Perceptions sometimes shift rapidly on

Wednesday afternoon, the last day of the 14 day reserve accounting period. Figure 8 shows a case in which the supply of reserves exceeds the demand for reserves.

Depository institutions have more non-borrowed reserves than they need hence the funds rate would fall sharply. In April 1979, for example, the rate fell from double-digit levels to 2 percent in one day.

Open market operations are carried out by the Federal Reserve Bank of New York under the direction of the Federal Open Market Committee (FOMC). The voting members of the FOMC are the seven members of the Board of Governors of the Federal Reserve System, the President of the Federal Reserve Bank of New York, and four of the Presidents from the other eleven Federal Reserve Banks who serve on the FOMC on a rotational basis. The FOMC meet in Washington, D. C. about every six weeks to assess the current economic outlook. The FOMC votes on intermediate policy objectives and issues a directive to the trading desk manager of open market operations in the New York Federal Reserve Bank. The directive stipulates the target fed funds rate.

Further Discussion of Inelasticity

The fed funds rate can be very volatile because the market for reserves is inelastic in the very short run. The banking system has no immediate way to rid itself of excess reserves. A system-wide excess of reserves would push the funds rate to zero. Even if banks were able to increase their volume of lending, excess reserves would persist. Within the current accounting period each new loan creates a deposit somewhere in the banking system, but each new loan absorbs only a tiny fraction of the excess reserves. Furthermore, lending decisions are generally independent of reserve needs.

With a system-wide shortage of reserves the Fed is the only source of immediate funds. In the extreme, banks short of their reserve requirement fail if unable to acquire the required reserves. Faced with imminent failure banks would bid up the funds rate trying to borrow from each other. As the funds rate rose more banks would go to the discount window. Banks may try to reduce their reserve requirement by reducing the volume of their outstanding loans. However, forcing the repayment of loans is an ineffective method of meeting reserve requirements within the banking system. When a bank is deficient by, say $10,000, a $10,000 loan may be called in to increase the amount of reserves by $10,000. However, the loan repayment lowers the deposits in another bank. The deficiency has merely shifted from one bank to another. Repayment of loans reduces the reserve requirement only marginally within the banking system. A huge reduction in the volume of outstanding loans brings about only a small reduction in the banking systems' total reserve requirement. Reserve positions must be settled immediately not months later. The banking system can obtain reserves on a day-to-day basis from only one source, the Fed. Within a given accounting period the banking system has no other practical means of reducing its reserve requirement by a significant amount.

Lead Accounting

Out of a more desperate quest for control of total reserves emerges the concept of lead accounting. The concept is more of an academic ideal than a workable proposition. In a lead accounting system the maintenance period would actually be prior to the computation period. Such a system would result in a very restrictive and highly unstable environment. A reserve deficiency under a lead accounting system could be more accurately labeled a deposit excess. In such a case the banking system would have to undergo drastic changes in its loan portfolio. A single bank may have a small degree of latitude to adjust its loan portfolio in order to meet its reserve requirement. For example, if Bank A has a $10 million reserve deficiency, and if it were able to force repayment of $10 million of loans, Bank A's reserve balance would increase by the needed $10 million. However, the loan repayment reduces the deposits in other banks by $10 million. By calling in loans Bank A has not eliminated the reserve deficiency but merely transferred the deficiency to other banks. When banks call loans the amount of total deposits in the banking system declines, but the reduction of total deposits reduces the amount of required reserves only marginally. The reserve requirement is one- tenth of the total deposits; a large reduction in the amount of total deposits would cause only a small reduction in the level of required reserves. The words "call in loans" roll easily off the word processor, but what does this imply? First, the portion of outstanding loans which are callable is small. Therefore, the U.S. banking system does not have the immediate ability to expand or contract deposits to meet short-term reserve requirements. Second, forcing changes in loan portfolios through lead accounting would inflict a sever disruption and unnecessary volatility, as individuals and firms would be forced to sell off assets to reduce their borrowing on a day's notice, regardless of their equity or credit standing.

The desire to implement lead reserve accounting is a rash reaction to the Central Bank's lack of direct control of total bank reserves. It is a banking version of the mountain moving to Mohammed. Even if lead reserve accounting were enacted its effect would be far too disruptive to be used. The Federal Reserve's use of lead accounting methods to control bank lending would be like a local police force using tactical nuclear weapons to quell a domestic disturbance. In either case, the power of the corrective action is so grossly disproportionate to the situation that it is unusable.

More on Why Lead Accounting is Unworkable – Inelasticity for Loan Demand

Financial intermediation has developed into a sophisticated and essential institution in the modern economy. Lending is a practical reality of economic growth and the demand for loans is very inelastic in the very short run. Even as interest rates change the volume of outstanding loans adjusts on the margin, gradually. Many loans have a fixed rate and are not affected by interest rate changes. In the long run, loan demand and thus reserve demand, become somewhat more elastic as individuals and businesses respond to interest rate changes.

Many commodities share the property of short-run inelasticity. That is the demand for these goods does not change with a change in the price of the good. Consider, for example, a group of scuba divers' demand for air. If the divers were down to their last few breaths of air and were unable to surface they would surely be willing to pay any price for a tank of air. The only options for the divers are buy more air or perish. The imaginary seller of air would be able to set any price for his air. The quantity of air, however, depends entirely on what the divers need. Once the divers have enough air additional air is of no value. The buyers determine the quantity, and the seller sets the price. The inelasticity of the banking system's demand for reserves is somewhat analogous to the inelastic demand for a scuba divers air.

The Federal Reserve can set the price of reserves but the quantity is determined by the banking system. The market for reserves is not perfectly inelastic because the Fed allows some spill-over in the accounting of bank reserves from one period to the next. This practice allows banks to smooth out some of the volatility of their reserve positions but it does not change the inelastic nature of the market for reserves. Efforts to force the market to accept fewer loans than are demanded would be nearly as disruptive as forcing the divers to make do with no air. The banking system would have to reduce their outstanding loans by forcing customers to immediately sell off assets financed through the banking system. The senseless dislocation of assets caused by forced disintermediation makes such an action unthinkable. Central bankers who understand the intractable nature of the banking system's loan portfolio recognize the necessity of lagged reserve accounting. A sensible approach to changing the money supply employs a change in the fed funds rate to gradually bring about the desired result.

What if No One Buys the Debt

It is not possible to adequately address every question raised by "debt phoebes". One of the most common concerns, however, clearly illustrates the unfounded fear that arises from confusing private borrowing with public borrowing. The question is based on an image of Uncle Sam being turned away by lenders and being stuck without financing.

Fear the government will be unable to sell securities overlooks the mechanics of the process itself. The imperative of borrowing is interest rate support. By issuing government securities, the government offers banks an opportunity to exchange non-interest bearing reserves for interest bearing securities. If all banks would rather earn zero interest on their assets than accept interest payments from the government, the refusal to accept interest becomes a de facto tax on the banking system. From the Treasury's point of view the government's inability to attract any lenders would actually be a benefit. Imagine, the government spends money and the banking system, in a sense, lends the money at zero interest by refusing to accept interest on the new deposits which the government spending created. Instead, the banking system is content to leave the money in a non-interest bearing account at the Fed. The money is held at the Fed either way - it has no other existence. If the money is left as excess reserves it sits in a non-interest bearing account at the Fed. If the money is loaned to the government by purchasing government securities it again is held at the government's account at the Fed.

How the Government Spends and Borrows as Much as it Does Without Causing Hyperinflation

Most people are accustomed to viewing savings from their own individual point of view. It can be difficult to think of savings on the national level. Putting part of one's salary into a savings account means only that an individual has not spent all of his income. The effect of not spending as such is to reduce the demand for consumption below what would have been if the income which is saved had been spent. The act of saving will reduce effective demand for current production without necessarily bringing about any compensating increase in the demand for investment. In fact, a decrease in effective demand most likely reduces employment and income. Attempts to increase individual savings may actually cause a decrease in national income, a reduction in investment, and a decrease in total national savings. One person's savings can become another's pay cut.

Savings equals investment. If investment doesn't change, one person's savings will necessarily be matched by another's' dissaving's. Every credit has an offsetting debit.

As one firm's expenses are another person's income, spending equal to a firm's expenses is necessary to purchase its output. A shortfall of consumption results in an increase of unsold inventories. When business inventories accumulate because of poor sales: 1) businesses may lower their production and employment and 2) business may invest in less new capital. Businesses often invest in order to increase their productive capacity and meet greater demand for their goods. Chronically low demand for consumer goods and services may depress investment and leaves businesses with over capacity and reduce investment expenditures. Low spending can put the economy in the doldrums: low sales, low income, low investment, and low savings.

When demand is strong and sales are high businesses normally respond by increasing output. They may also invest in additional capital equipment. Investment in new capacity is automatically an increase in savings. Savings rises because workers are paid to produce capital goods they cannot buy and consume. The only other choice left is for individuals to "invest" in capital goods, either directly or through an intermediary. An increase in investment for whatever reason is an increase in savings; a decrease in individual spending, however, does not cause an increase in overall investment.

> **SAVINGS EQUALS INVESTMENT, BUT THE ACT OF INVESTMENT MUST OCCUR TO HAVE REAL SAVINGS.**

The relationship between individual spending decisions and national income is illustrated by assuming the flow of money is through the banking system. The money businesses pay their workers may either be used to buy their output or deposited in a bank. If the money is deposited in a bank, the bank has two basic lending options. The money can be loaned to: 1) someone else who wishes to purchase the output (including the government), or 2) to businesses who paid the individuals in the first place for the purpose of financing the unsold output. If the general demand for goods declines the demand for loans to finance inventories rises. If, on the other hand, individuals spent money at a high rate the demand for purchase loans would rise, inventories would decline and the level of loans to finance business inventories would fall.

The structural situation in the U. S. is one in which individuals are given powerful incentives not to spend. This has allowed the government, in a sense, to spend people's money for them. The reason that government deficit spending has not resulted in more inflation is that it has offset a structurally reduced rate of private spending. A large portion of personal income consists of IRA contributions, Keoghs, life insurance reserves, pension fund income, and other money that compounds continuously and is not spent. Similarly, a significant portion of business income is also low velocity; it accumulates in corporate savings accounts of various types. Dollars earned by foreign central banks are also not likely to be spent.

The root of this paradox is the mistaken notion that savings is needed to provide money for investment. This is not true. In the banking system, loans, including those for business investments, create equal deposits, obviating the need for savings as a source of money. Investment creates its own money.

Once we recognize that savings does not cause investment it follows that the solution to high unemployment and low capacity utilization is not necessarily to encourage more savings. In fact, taxed advantaged savings has probably caused the private sector to desire to be a NET saver. This condition requires the public sector to run a deficit, or face deflation.

Full Employment and Price Stability

There is a very interesting fiscal policy option that is not under consideration, because it may result in a larger budget deficit. The Federal government could offer a job to anyone who applies, at a fixed rate of pay, and let the deficit float. This would result in full employment, by definition. It would also eliminate the need for such legislation as unemployment compensation and a minimum wage.

This new class of government employees, which could be called supplementary, would function as an automatic stabilizer, the way unemployment currently does. A strong economy with rising labor costs would result in supplementary employees leaving their government jobs, as the private sector lures them with higher wages. (The government must allow this to happen, and not increases wages to compete.) This reduction of government expenditures is a contractionary fiscal bias. If the economy slows, and workers are laid off from the private sector, they will immediately assume supplementary government employment. The resulting increase in government expenditures is an expansionary bias. As long as the government does not change the supplementary wage, it becomes the defining factor for the currency- the price around which free market prices in the private sector evolve.

> **ONCE THE GOVERNMENT LEVIES A TAX, THE PRIVATE SECTOR NEEDS THE GOVERNMENT'S MONEY SO THAT IT CAN PAY THE TAX.**

A government using fiat money has pricing power that it may not understand. The conventional understanding that the government must tax so it can get money to spend does not apply to a fiat currency. Because the private sector needs the government's money to meet its tax obligations, the government can literally name its price for the money it spends. In a market economy it is only necessary to define one price and let the market establish the rest. For this example I am proposing to set the price of the supplementary government workers.

This is not meant to be a complete analysis. It is meant to illustrate the point that there are fiscal options that are not under consideration because of the fear of deficits.

Taxation

Taxation is part of the process of obtaining the resources needed by the government. The government has an infinite amount of its fiat currency to spend. Taxes are needed to get the private sector to trade real goods and services in return for the fiat money it needs to pay taxes. From the government's point of view, it is a matter of price times quantity equals revenue.

Given this, the secondary effects of taxes can now be considered before deciding on the tax structure. A sales tax will inhibit transactions, as will an income tax. This tendency to restrict trade and transactions is generally considered a detriment. It reduces the tendency to realize the benefits of specialization of labor and comparative advantage. Furthermore, transaction taxes offer large rewards for successful evasion, and therefore require powerful enforcement agencies and severe penalties. They also result in massive legal efforts to transact without being subject to the taxes as defined by the law. Add this to the cost of all of the record keeping necessary to be in compliance. All of these are real economic costs of transactions taxes.

A real estate tax is an interesting alternative. It is much easier to enforce, provides a more stable demand for government spending, and does not discourage transactions. It can be made progressive, if the democracy desires.

How much money one has may be less important than how much one spends. This is not a common consideration. But having money does not consume real resources. Nor does one person's accumulation of nominal wealth preclude another's, since the quantity of money available is infinite. Fiat money is only a tax credit.

Perhaps those in favor of a progressive tax system should instead be concerned over the disproportionate consumption of real resources. Rather than attempting to tax away one's money at source, luxury taxes could be levied to prevent excess consumption (not to raise revenue). The success of the luxury tax should be measured by how little money it raises.

Foreign Trade

By the tenor of recent trade discussions it is apparent that the modern world has forgotten that exports are the cost of imports. Under a gold standard, each transaction was more clearly defined. If one imported cars, and paid in currency, the cars had been exchanged for gold. Cars were imported and gold was exported. Fiat money changed this. If a nation imports cars, and pays in its own fiat currency, cars are still imported but no commodity is exported. The holder of that money has a very loosely defined currency. In fact, the holder of currency is only guaranteed to be able to buy something from a willing seller at the seller's offered price. Any country running a trade surplus is taking risk inherent in accumulating fiat foreign currency. Real goods and services are leaving the country running a surplus, in return for an uncertain ability to import in the future. The importing country is getting real goods and services, and agreeing only to later export at whatever price it pleases to other countries holding its currency. That means that if the United States suddenly put a tax on exports, Japan's purchasing power would be reduced.

Inflation vs. Price Increase

Little or no consideration has been given to the possibility that higher prices may simply be the market allocating resources and not inflation.

Prices reflect the indifference levels where buyers and sellers meet. The market mechanism allows the participants to make their purchases and sales at any price on which they mutually agree. Market prices tend to change continuously. If, for example, there is a freeze in Brazil, the price of coffee may go up. The higher price accommodates the transfer of the remaining supply of coffee from the sellers to the buyers.

Prices going up and down can be the market allocating resources, not a problem of inflation. Inflation is the process whereby the government causes higher prices by creating more money either directly through deficit spending, or indirectly by lowering interest rates or otherwise encouraging borrowing. For example, when a shortage of goods and services causes higher prices, a government may attempt to help its constituents to buy more by giving them more money. Of course, a shortage means that the desired products don't exist. More money just raises the price. When that, in turn, causes the government to further increase the money available, an inflationary spiral has been created. The institutionalization of this process is called indexing.

Left alone, the price of coffee, gold, or just about anything may go up, down, or sideways. Goods and services go through cycles. One year, there may be a record harvest and the next a disaster. Oil can be in shortage one decade, and then in surplus the next. There could, conceivably, be years, or even decades when the CPI grows at, say, 5% without any real inflation. There may be fewer things to go around, with the market allocating them to the highest bidder.

As the economy expands and the population increases, some items in relatively fixed supply are bound to gain value relative to items in general supply. Specifically, gold, waterfront property, and movie star retainers will likely increase relative to computers, watches, and other electronics.

If the Fed should decide to manage the economy by targeting the price of gold, they would respond to an increase in the price of gold with higher interest rates. The purpose would be to discourage lending, thereby reducing money creation. In effect, the Fed would try to reduce the amount of money we all have in order to keep the price of gold down. That may then depress the demand for all other goods and services, even though they may be in surplus. By raising rates, the Fed is saying that there is too much money in the economy and it is causing a problem.

Presumably there is some advantage to targeting gold, the CPI, or any other index, rather than leaving the money alone and letting the market adjust prices. Interest rates can be too low and lead to excess money creation relative to the goods and services available for sale. On the other hand, higher commodity prices may represent the normal ebbs and flows in the markets for these items.

If there are indeed price increases due to changing supply dynamics, Fed policy of restricting money may result in a slowdown of serious proportions which would not have occurred if they had left interest rates alone.

Conclusion

The supposed technical and financial limits imposed by the federal budget deficit and federal debt are a vestige of commodity money. Today's fiat currency system has no such restrictions. The concept of a financial limit to the level of untaxed federal spending (money creation/deficit spending) is erroneous. The former constraints imposed by the gold standard have been gone since 1971. This is not to say that deficit spending does not have economic consequences. It is to say that the full range of fiscal policy options should be considered and evaluated based on their economic impacts rather than imaginary financial restraints. Current macroeconomic policy can center on how to more fully utilize the nation's productive resources. True overcapacity is an easy problem to solve. We can afford to employ idle resources.

Obsolete economic models have hindered our ability to properly address real issues. Our attention has been directed away from issues which have real economic effects to meaningless issues of accounting. Discussions of income, inflation, and unemployment have been overshadowed by the national debt and deficit. The range of possible policy actions has been needlessly restricted. Errant thinking about the federal deficit has left policy makers unwilling to discuss any measures which might risk an increase in the amount of federal borrowing. At the same time they are increasing savings incentives, which create further need for those unwanted deficits.

The major economic problems facing the United States today are not extreme. Only a misunderstanding of money and accounting prevents Americans from achieving a higher quality of life that is readily available.

Mosler Speech - Rome Debt Management Conference October 26, 2012

I'll first address what I believe is the most misunderstood question, which is why the euro national governments debts are as high as they are. The answer begins with the absolute fact that government debt is equal to global 'non-government' accumulations of euro financial assets. For any given 'closed sector' the euro is a traditional case of 'inside money', as with a 'giro' or 'clearing house.' The only way an agent could have net euro financial assets would be for another to be net borrowed. For every euro asset there is a euro liability. The net is always zero.

This type of system famously can't accommodate a net desire to save, unless there is a provision for net financial assets to enter the sector in question. In the case of the euro, this means the non-government sector requires government deficit spending to satisfy its net savings desires, should there be any. Additionally, note that all government spending is either used to pay taxes or remains as net savings in the economy, in one form or another. And unemployment, as defined, is the evidence that the economy does not have sufficient euro income to pay its taxes and fulfill its net savings desires.

The answer to why national government debt is so high continues with an investigation of the 'savings desires' that generate the need for net financial assets. European institutional structure includes powerful incentives to not spend income, and to instead accumulate financial assets. Historically these have been called 'demand leakages', and include tax advantaged as well as mandatory requirements for income to go into retirement funds, corporate reserves, as well as actual cash in circulation. Without an equal expansion of private sector debt by other agents spending more than their incomes, these savings desires can't be realized, unless governments spend more than their income.

In the years immediately before the euro, the member nations with today's high debts had their own currencies. As currency issuers, whether they realized it or not, they had no solvency issues, they set their own interest rates, and they accommodated domestic savings desires with government deficit spending, which allowed them to sustain growth and keep unemployment relatively low.

The point here is that high deficits were offsetting the high demand leakages built into the institutional structures. And that requirement has not gone away, as the traditional demand leakages remain. And note that the nation with the lowest deficit, Luxemburg, never had its own currency, and instead market forces caused them to fund their net financial assets with net exports.

What changed with the euro, and the 'divorces' from the national central banks, was the ability to fund national deficits. The euro nation's financial dynamics became very much like the US states. They can no longer 'print the money', and are instead revenue constrained. However, the difference is that, unlike the US states, the euro members entered the euro with the higher debt levels incurred when they were issuers of their currencies, not constrained by revenues, and acting to offset demand leakages as required to sustain output and employment.

Today, the ECB is the central bank for the euro. I often call it the 'score keeper' for the euro. The ECB system spends and lends euro simply by crediting accounts. These euro don't 'come from' anywhere.

They are 'data entry'. As Chairman Bernanke responded when asked where the hundreds of billions of dollars lent to the banks came from: '...we simply use the computer to mark up the size of the account they have with the Fed.'

In fact, any central bank, operationally, can make any size payments in its own currency. When the ECB makes a 500 million euro securities purchase, no one asks where the euro came from, whether it was taxpayer money, or whether the ECB somehow borrowed it from China. Central banks are not revenue constrained in their own currency. This puts them in the unique position of being able to act counter cyclically during a down turn in the economy.

Conversely, the euro members, like the US states, are not financially capable of reacting counter cyclically to increased savings desires when private sector credit expansion fails and economies slow.

Only the ECB can, as I like to say, 'write the check' to allow for the provision of the net financial assets demanded by the institutional structure, as evidenced by the rate of unemployment and the output gap in general.

Given the state of private sector credit and net export potential, the euro zone currently needs even higher levels of government deficit spending than otherwise to sustain growth and employment. And only the ECB can write that check. And yes, I realize the political difficulties this implies, the most pressing issue being that of moral hazard.

Given the necessity of more national government debt and with only the ECB ultimately capable of writing the check, I'll now discuss policy options for closing the output gap, and their associated risks.

A simple ECB guarantee of national government debt and an expansion of Maastricht limits to perhaps 7% of GDP would trigger an immediate surge of sales, output, employment, and general prosperity.

However, without adequate enforcement of limits, it would also surely trigger an inflationary race to the bottom, as the nation managing to run the largest deficits would benefit the most in real terms. So the challenge is to allow the right level of fiscal expansion to accommodate the demand leakages of the independent member nations, but without the direct central fiscal control of a currency union like the US.

Tax credit bonds are another option. These are bonds that have the same characteristics of today's sovereign debt, but in the case of non-payment (there is no default condition) these fully transferrable bonds can be used for payment of taxes to the government of issue. This means that taxpayers of other members will never be asked to pay any other member's obligations, which I presume would have wide political appeal.

A third option is for the ECB to make 'cash' distributions to the member nations on a per capita basis of perhaps 10% of euro zone GDP annually. This would begin a systematic reduction of member deficits towards zero over a multi-year period. It would also have to include strict spending limits to regulate aggregate demand. To that end, the ECB could withhold payment to violators, which is far easier to do than imposing and collecting fines, as is the case today.

Twenty years ago I was in Rome at the finance ministry meeting with Professor Luigi Spaventa, along with my colleague Maurice Samuels of Harvard Management. Those, too, were dark days for Italy. Debt was over 100% of GDP, interest rates over 12%, the global economy was weak, and Professor Rudi Dornbusch had been making the rounds proclaiming that Italian default was certain. I asked Professor Spaventa, rhetorically, why Italy was issuing CCT's and

BTP's. Was it to fund expenditures, or was it because if the treasury spent the lira, and did not issue securities, and the Bank of Italy did not sell securities, the overnight rate would fall to 0? There was a long pause before Professor Spaventa answered 'no, rates would only fall to ½% as we pay interest on reserves' indicating full and sudden understanding that there was no default risk. He then immediately rose with an attack on IMF conditionality. A great weight had been lifted. The next week it was announced 'no extraordinary measures would be taken - all payments will be met on time" and the debt crisis receded.

Solving that debt crisis was relatively easy, as in fact there was no debt crisis. Today the situation is both more serious and more complex. The economic problem is that deficits are too small, while the political understanding is that deficits are too large. And the consequential ECB funding with conditionality translates into lower rates and higher unemployment.

Note that I have made no mention of interest rates or monetary policy in general. My 40 years of experience as an insider in monetary operations tells me they matter very little for growth and employment. And for nations with high deficits, I've come to expect high rates from the CB to function to promote inflation from both the interest income channels, and through the general cost structure of the economy.

I will conclude with very brief word on inflation. Just like the dollar, yen, and pound, the euro is a simple public monopoly. And any monopolist is necessarily price setter, not price taker.

Furthermore, a monopolist sets two prices. First is what Marshall called the 'own rate' which is how the monopolist's thing exchanges for itself. For a currency that is the interest rate set by the CB.

The second is how that thing exchanges for other goods and services. For a currency we call that the price level. I say it this way - the price level is necessarily a function of prices paid by the government of issue when it spends, and/or collateral demanded when it lends.

What this means for the euro zone is that inflation control ultimately comes down to limiting government spending by limiting selected prices member nations are allowed to pay when they spend.

> **LIKE CENTRAL BANKING, IT'S ABOUT PRICE, AND NOT QUANTITY.**

Thank you.

Other Recommended Books

Randall Wray, <u>Modern Money Theory</u>

Randall Wray, <u>Understanding Modern Money</u>

William Black, <u>The Best way to Rob a bank is to Own One</u>

Appendix for Soft Currency Economics

Charts used in Soft Currency Economics

Figure 1 - The Lagged Reserve Accounting System, 1968-1984
Figure 2 - The lagged Reserve Accounting System, 1984 to present
Figure 3 - The Government Spends $500 million and Taxes $500 million
Figure 4 - The Government Spends $500 million and borrows $500
Figure 5 - Probabilities of the Open Market Desk Daily Transactions June 1998 to December 1990
Figure 6 - Likelihood that the Fed's Desk uses Repurchase and Reverse Repos
Figure 7 - Supply and demand curve for Reserves
Figure 8 - Supply and Demand Curves for Reserves

Bibliography for Soft Currency Economics

Auerbach, Robert D., Money, Banking, and Financial Markets, 2nd Ed., MacMillian, 1985.
Berstein, Peter L., A Primer on Money, Banking, and Gold, Vintage Books, 1965.
Board of Governors of the Federal Reserve System, The Federal Reserve System: Purposes and Functions, 7th Ed. (The Board 1984).
Bryant, Ralph C.,"Controlling Money", The Brookings Institution, 1983.
Cosimano, Thomas F. and John B. Van Huyck,"Dynamic Monetary Control and Interest Rate Stabilization", Journal of Monetary Economics 23, 1989, pp. 53-63.
Dillard, Dudley, The Economics of John Maynard Keynes, The Theory of a Monetary Economy, (New York: Prentice-Hall, 1948).
Feige, Edgar L., Robert McGee, "Money Supply Control and Lagged Reserve Accounting", Journal of Money, Credit, and Banking, Vol. 9 (November 1977), pp. 536-551.
Feinman, Joshua N., "Reserve Requirements: History, Current Practice, and Potential Reform", Federal Reserve Bulletin, June 1993, pp. 569-589.
Feinman, Joshua N., "Estimating the Open Market Desk's Daily Reaction Fraction", Journal of Money, Credit, and Banking, Vol. 25, No 2 (May 1993).
Henning, Charles N., Pigott, William, Scott, Robert Haney, Financial Markets and the Economy, 4th Ed., Prentice-Hall, 1984.
Knodell, Jane, "Open Market Operations: Evolution and Significance", Journal of Economic Issues, (June 1987), pp. 691-699.
Laurent, Robert D., "Lagged Reserve Accounting and the Fed's New Operating Procedure", Economic Perspectives, Federal Reserve Bank of Chicago, Midyear 1982, pp. 32-44.
Manypenny, Gerald D. and Bermudez, Michael L., "The Federal Reserve Banks as Fiscal Agents and Depositories of the United States", Federal Reserve Bulletin, October, 1992.
Mayer, Thomas, Duesenberry, James S., Aliber, Robert Z., Money, Banking, and the Economy, 2nd Ed., W.W. Norton & Company, 1984.
McDonough, William, et al, "Desk Activity for the Open Market Account", Federal Reserve Bank of New York, Quarterly Review, Spring 1992-93, pp. 109-114.

Meulendyke, Ann-Marie, "Reserve Requirements and the Discount Window in Recent Decades", Federal Reserve Bank of New York, Quarterly Review, Vol. 17 (Autumn 1992).

Meyer, Lawerence H., Editor, "Improving Money Stock Control", Center for the Study of American Business, (Boston: Kluwer-Nijhoff Publishing, 1983).

Mishkin, Frederic S., The Economics of Money, Banking, and Financial Markets, 3rd Ed., Harper Collins, 1992.

Pierce, David A.,"Money Supply Control: Reserves as the Instrument Under Lagged Accounting", The Journal of Finance, Vol. XXXI, No. 3 (June 1976) pp. 845-852.

Rosenbaum, Mary Susan, "Contemporaneous Reserve Accounting: The New System and Its Implications for Monetary Policy", Economic Review, Federal Reserve Bank of Atlanta (April 1984), pp. 46-57.

Roth, Howard L., "Federal Reserve Open Market Techniques", Economic Review, Federal Reserve Bank of Kansas City (March 1986).

Timberlake, Richard H., "Institutional Evolution of Federal Reserve Hegemony", Cato Journal, Vol. 5, No. 3 (Winter 1986).

About the Author

What others are saying about Warren Mosler:

"**One of the brightest minds in finance**." CNBC (6/11/10)

"Warren Mosler is one of the most original and clear-eyed participants in today's debates over economic policy." **JAMES GALBRAITH, FORMER EXECUTIVE DIRECTOR, JOINT ECONOMIC COMMITTEE AND PROFESSOR, THE UNIVERSITY OF TEXAS – AUSTIN**

"In this model of clarity, Warren Mosler debunks (in his own words) so many of the 'innocent frauds' that have contributed to our current economic and social malaise. More importantly, Mosler is no Ivory Tower academic. He has been a highly successful money manager, and his characterization of our modern monetary system is spot on: Mosler far more accurately depicts market realities than any of the self-styled "mainstream" economics textbooks, which dominate in the halls of academe, and in the corridors of power in Washington, Brussels, and Asia. This book should not only become mandatory reading for students of economics, but any policy maker who truly wants to deal with the grave disasters engendered from years of "reading from the wrong playbook" **MARSHALL AUERBACK, DIRECTOR INSTITUTE FOR NEW ECONOMIC THINKING, PINETREE CAPITAL**

PORTFOLIO STRATEGIST, FELLOW FOR THE ECONOMISTS FOR PEACE AND SECURITY, RESEARCH ASSOCIATE, LEVY INSTITUTE.

"I can say without hesitation that Warren Mosler has had the most profound impact on our understanding of modern money and government budgets of anyone I know or know of, including Nobel Prize winners, Central Bank Directors, Ministers of Finance and full professors at Ivy League Universities. It is no exaggeration to say that his ideas concerning economic theory and policy are responsible for the most exciting new paradigm in economics in the last 30 years - perhaps longer - and he has inspired more economists to turn their attention to the real world of economic policy than any other single individual." **DR. MATTHEW FORSTATER, PROFESSOR OF ECONOMICS, UNIVERSITY OF MISSOURI - KANSAS CITY**

"Warren is one of the rare individuals who understand money and finance and how the Treasury and the Fed really work. He receives information from industry experts from all over the world." **WILLIAM K. BLACK, ASSOCIATE PROFESSOR OF ECONOMICS & LAW, UNIVERSITY OF MISSOURI - KANSAS CITY**

Warren Mosler is a world renowned financier, economist and entrepreneur. For Mosler, life has always been about the intellectual challenge of reducing seemingly complex phenomena to their simplest terms in the chase for the "elegant solution".

As a financier, Mosler is the co-founder of Illinois Income Investors (III), a family of leveraged fixed income investment funds. He developed numerous successful strategies that utilized US Government securities, mortgage backed securities, LIBOR swaps and LIBOR caps, and financial markets in a market neutral, zero duration strategy. Mosler originated the 'mortgage swap' in 1986 and orchestrated the largest futures delivery to date (over $20 billion notional) in Japan in 1996. He is also the inventor of a swap futures contract currently in operation (in a muted form) by a major exchange. III was rated number by MAR in risk adjusted returns for the prior 10 years in 1997 when he returned control over to his partners.

Warren Mosler is currently the Present of Valance Co, Inc. located in St. Croix in the US Virgin Islands, where he resides. Mosler is also Chairman and majority shareholder of Consulier Engineering (CSLR), President and founder of Mosler Automotive, which manufactures the MT900 sports car in Riviera Beach, Florida; Co-Founder and Distinguished Research Associate of The Center for Full Employment And Price Stability at the University of Missouri in Kansas City; Senior Associate Fellow, Cambridge Center for Economic and Public Policy, Downing College, Cambridge, UK; and Associate Fellow, University of Newcastle, Australia.

As an economist, Mosler has been about designing economic programs to achieve full employment and price stability in the United States. After the economic crash in 2008, Mosler proposed economic programs to help reduce unemployment and improve the economy through the stimulation of aggregate demand. These included temporary elimination of the payroll tax, a pro-rata funding for states and a guaranteed job program. In 2010, at the request of Independent Party, he ran for the Connecticut Senate seat on these issues. He finished third, but in many ways he won, because the Administration picked up and temporally implement a payroll tax cut.